Greetings, pigs!

MARVELS ANIMALS 51

PIGS

QUINN M. ARNOLD

CREATIVE EDUCATION | CREATIVE PAPERBACKS

I SMELL FREEDOM!

table of contents

Published by Creative Education and Creative Paperbacks
P.O. Box 227, Mankato, Minnesota 56002
Creative Education and Creative Paperbacks
are imprints of The Creative Company
www.thecreativecompany.us

Design by Wyeth Morgan
Art direction by Blue Design (www.bluedes.com)

Images by Alamy Stock Photo/1Apix, 14–15, nagelestock.com, cover (right), 17; Dreamstime/Isselee, 24, Sasilsolutions, 2, Thedreamstock, 18–19, Volodymyr Byrdyak, 8–9; Getty Images/Digital Zoo, 10–11, GK Hart/Vikki Hart, 20–21, Matt Carr, 4, Monty Rakusen, 6–7; iStock/AscentXmedia, 16; Pexels/Magda Ehlers, 13; Shutterstock/Catherine Eckert, 1, Tsekhmister, 3; Unsplash/Christopher Carson, 23, Matthieu Pétiard, cover (middle); Wikimedia Commons/public domain, cover (left)

Library of Congress Cataloging-in-Publication Data
Names: Arnold, Quinn M., author.
Title: Pigs / Quinn M. Arnold.
Description: Mankato, Minnesota : Creative Education / Creative Paperbacks, [2026] | Series: Marvels | Includes bibliographical references and index. | Audience: Ages 4-7 | Audience: Grades K-1 | Summary: "An introduction to pigs, this beginning reader features eye-catching photographs, humorous captions, and basic life science facts about these mud-loving mammals. Includes a labeled image guide, glossary, and further resources"– Provided by publisher.
Identifiers: LCCN 2024044735 (print) | LCCN 2024044736 (ebook) | ISBN 9798889895763 (library binding) | ISBN 9781682777480 (paperback) | ISBN 9798889895824 (ebook)
Subjects: LCSH: Swine–Juvenile literature.
Classification: LCC SF395.5 .A76 2026 (print) | LCC SF395.5 (ebook) | DDC 636.4–dc23/eng/20241213
LC record available at https://lccn.loc.gov/2024044735
LC ebook record available at https://lccn.loc.gov/2024044736

Printed in India

Short-legged pigs live on farms. Many stay in pigpens. Others walk around fields.

WISH I HAD HANDS TO DIG WITH...

All pigs have big ears and small eyes. Most have curly tails, too. Flat **snouts** help pigs dig for food.

Pigs are good swimmers. Pigs like to be clean. But they also wallow in mud.

PIGS DON'T STAY CLEAN FOR LONG.

A pig will eat almost anything! Farmers feed pigs corn, grains, or slops. Some pigs dig up plants and worms to eat.

THIS IS MUCH BETTER THAN WORMS!

A **sow** makes a nest for her piglets. The baby pigs drink milk. They nap in the hay.

Smart pigs try to get out of their pen. They toss their heads and run in fields. They grunt and squeal. They sniff for food.

Farewell, pigs!

[Picture a Pig]

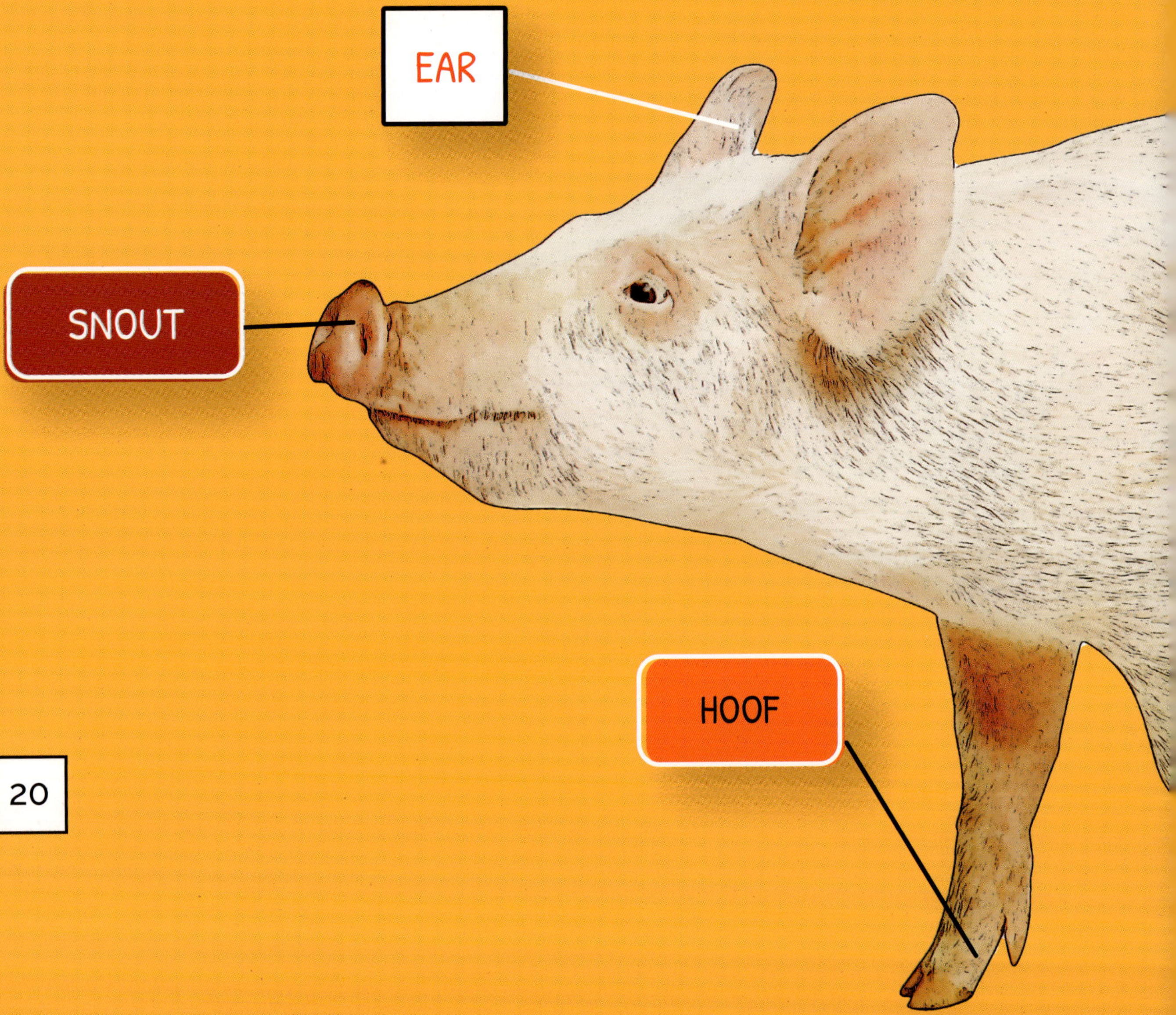

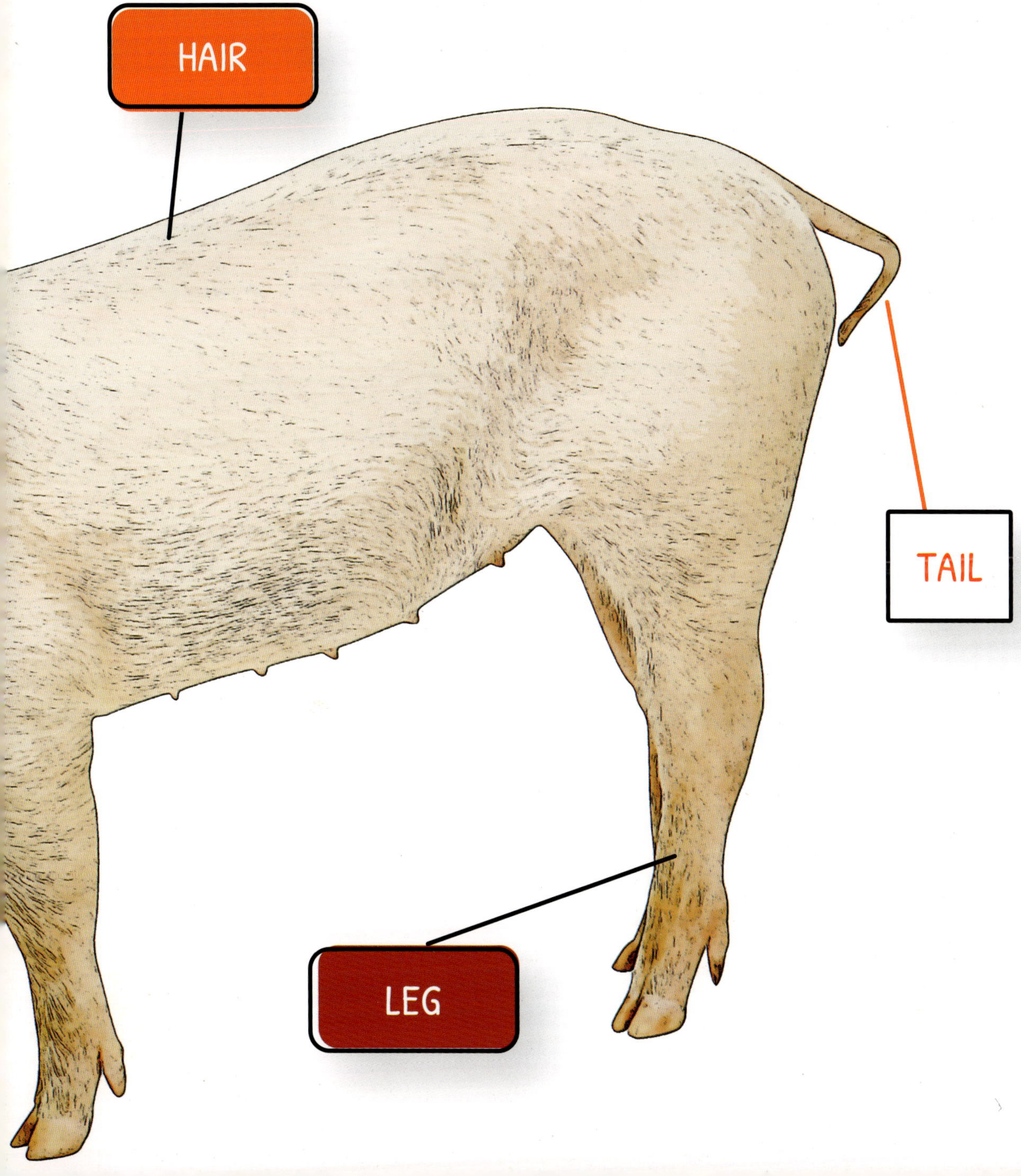
HAIR
TAIL
LEG

WORDS TO KNOW

slops: damaged fruits or vegetables, or leftover food scraps

snout: the nose and mouth of an animal that sticks out from its face

sow: a mother pig

wallow: to roll in dirt, mud, or water to keep cool and stop bugs from biting

READ MORE

Gottlieb, Beth. *I Love Pigs!* New York: Gareth Stevens Publishing, 2023.

Sabelko, Rebecca. *Pigs*. Minneapolis: Bellwether Media, 2024.

WEBSITES

Britannica Kids: Pig
https://kids.britannica.com/kids/article/pig/353626

Learn about different names for pigs and where they live.

National Geographic Kids: Pig
https://kids.nationalgeographic.com/animals/mammals/facts/pig

Read more about pigs.

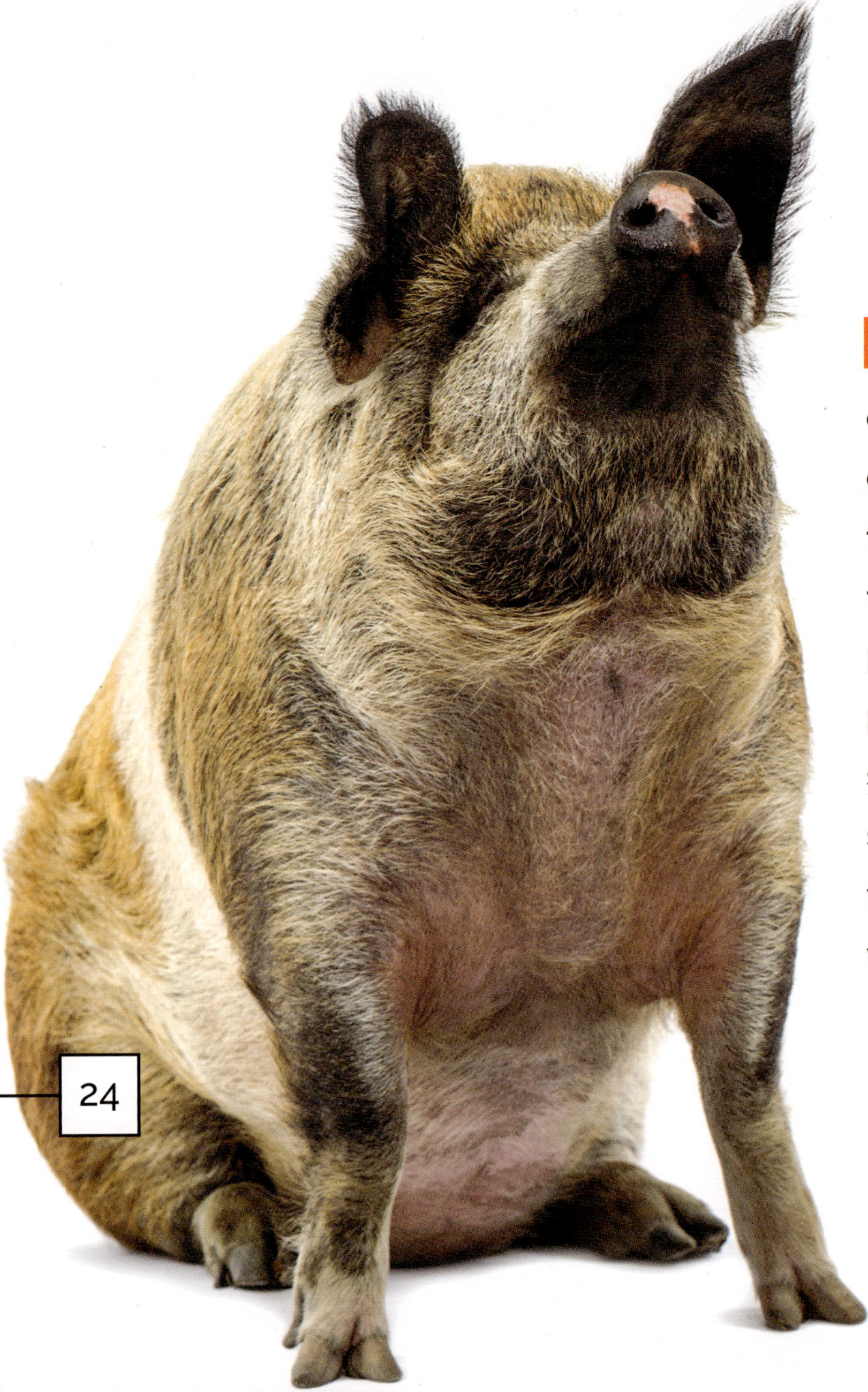

INDEX